Chiaroscúro

Louis A. Coppola

authorHOUSE®

AuthorHouse™
1663 Liberty Drive
Bloomington, IN 47403
www.authorhouse.com
Phone: 1-800-839-8640

First published by AuthorHouse 12/14/2009

ISBN: 978-1-4490-5705-3 (e)

ISBN: 978-1-4490-5706-0 (sc)

Printed in the United States of America
Bloomington, Indiana

This book is printed on acid-free paper.

Also by
Louis A. Coppola:

Essay-fiction Books

Homecrest Avenue, Silhouettes
of an Accidental Family

C.B.S, The Chucklehead
Broadcasting System

Television

Checkmate, ABC/TV,
The Benson Series

Chiaroscuro, by Louis A. Coppola, was presented by Double Image Theatre, May 12, 1978. Directed by the author; stage Manager, Susan Baylis; Assistant Stage Manager, Richard N. Coppola; Technical Coordinator, Charles Livermore; Production Super-visor, Helen Waren Mayer; Set Design, Louis A. Coppola.

CAST

Pop............................ Frank Nastasi
Tony.............................. Peter Gatto
Mom........................ Elaine Grollman
Magic.................... Barbara Campbell
Elwyn ....Michael Rogers

DESCRIPTION OF CHARACTERS

POP: Forty-five to sixty. Volatile Italian. Warm, earthy, loveable and theatrical.

TONY: Twenties, early thirties. Good looking. Warm, humorous, genuine, sensitive. Torn between his family and his needs.

MOM: Forties to fifties. More reflective than Pop, but doesn't pull her punches when she has a point to make.

MAGIC: Twenties. West Indian. Attractive. Complicated. Sensitive. torn between her own identity and her love for Tony.

ELWYN: Twenties to thirties. Magic's brother. Energetic, humorous. closer to his roots than Magic.

CHARACTERS

Tony
Pop, *his father.*
Mom, *Tony's mother.*
Magic, *Tony's girlfriend, a West Indian.*
Elwyn, *her brother.*

Time: *Saturday morning and Friday night,
shortly before Christmas.
Contemporary.*

Scenes: *A kitchen and a bedroom located in
different parts of the city.*

Chiaroscúro

Two playing levels. Front, Lower Level is the living room/bedroom. Down Left is the entrance. Several feet into the room is a bike exerciser. Down Right a divan; extreme R, a vanity, chair, and laundry basket. Stage Center, an Indian rug; Up L, an armchair; Up R, a side table, touch dial phone, a carnival hat, and chair.

The Rear, Upper level is the kitchen. A table, three chairs Center Left, several feet in from the platform edge to allow for playing area. Up Left is the bathroom; Up Center the back door; Up Right the kitchen entrance. The stove and sink extreme Right of the entrance; a garbage pail next to the stove. There are two windows, one above the sink, the other Down Center on a line with the table. The scene opens with partial light only in the kitchen. Pop enters in bathrobe and slippers.

Pop. (*Yawning broadly.*) Aye, Aye, Dio mio! (*Sets coffee to boil on stove.*)

Tony. (*Coming out of bathroom, towel in hand.*) What d'ya say, Pop?

Pop. (*Surprised.*) Eh? Toto? Is that you? (*Switches on overhead light.*)

Tony. Yeah. It's me.

Pop. (*Rapidly.*) You scare the life outa you father? I'm an old man. Let somebody know you comin'. What kind of a human bein' are you? Buon giorno. (*Beat.*) What-ah you doin' home?

Tony. I got lucky. Look, Pop. Sit down I wanna talk-

Pop. You left the back door open-ah. (*Closes door.*)

Tony. I thought the cat might go out.

Pop. That's you mother's cat.

Tony. Pop-

Pop. It's-ah her biz-ness. What-ah you wanna start, a revolution? Fatti i fatti tuoi! There's things you don't know, filgio mio. She took it to the, ah, come si dice? (*Strangulation gesture by crotch.*) Capisci? (*Slices air with hand.*)

Tony. (*Appalled.*) No!

Pop. Si. Non è buono per niente. It sits on the window like a mumma luca, starin' outside like he lost somethin', but what, he don't know. Eh! If it was for the women, caro mio, we'd all be sittin' on that window. Le donne sono la rovina del mondo!

Tony. Right. The ruination of the world. (*Places towel on back of center chair, and sits.*)

Pop. Bravo. Keep the back door closed. (*Entering bathroom.*) The only thing goin' out is the heat.

(*From within.*) Ma-donna! (*Returns, lighted match in one hand, fanning air with the other.*) Sei forte, *forte!* Must be your mother's side. You left the toilet seat up.

Tony. I'm using the bathroom.

Pop. Makes no difference. Always keep the toilet seat down!

Tony. Right. Next time I'll go to the park.

Pop. Somethin' falls in and clops up the pipes it's-a goodbye John-a.

Tony. Nothin'll fall in.

Pop. (*Whips out toothbrush, shoves it in TONY's face.*) See this? Forty dollars!

Tony. (*Momentarily stunned.*) Seventy-nine cents. My toothbrush.

Pop. (*Shaking it in* TONY's *face.*) Forty dollars! We give the plumber to find this clopped up in the pipes.

Tony. It was in the shithole and you kept it? (*Licking teeth, grimacing.*)

Pop. It's-a clean.

Tony. I used it.

Pop. I wash it in turpentine.

Tony. (*Grabs toothbrush.*) You don't throw nothin' out, do you? (*Throws it in pail by sink.*)

Pop. Comes the depression you'll thank you father.

Tony. Forget the depression!

Pop. Comes the depression even you own brother's a stranger.

Tony. Next time something goes wrong tell me. I'll pay for it.

Pop. Cosa?

Tony. (*Louder, rubbing two fingers.*) I'll pay for it!

Pop. You'll pay my a-eyes! You dreamin'. How you pay? With you mouth! Eh, you gotta reach. (*Indicates pocket.*)

Tony. I'll reach.

Pop. You don't even reach on Father's Day.

Tony. What're you talking about?

Pop. You reach for the telephone. Did you come visit you father on Father's Day? Your sisters came, even you brother upstairs, that chiacchieróne! They all pay the respect, but you (*Rubbing two fingers.*) niente! And you gonna reach for the plumber? Quando mai!

Tony. I'll give you five before I go.

Pop. Five? (*Crossing himself.*) Padre, Figlio, Spiritu, Santo.

Tony. I'm on strike. Remember?

Pop. It's nothin'. You go back with an increase.

Tony. Meanwhile I'm out with a decrease.

Pop. Now. Disgraziato! Last April you got back a *thousand* dollars from the tax.

Tony. You did open the mail.

Pop. (*(Rolling on.)* And I never once hear you say to you father, (*Crossing R. of Tony.*) "Pop. Here's a hundred dollars. Divertiti!"

Tony. A hundred?!

Pop. You only got one father!

Tony. But I haven't got one hundred.

Pop. Big shot-ah TV engineer-ree!

Tony. Radio. (*Rising.*) Look, Pop. I don't wanna argue money or a stinking toilet seat. I came over to talk about...

Pop. What-ah you do with all your money?

Tony. (*Exasperated.*) Eat it! (*Sits chair L.*)

Pop. (*Pursuing.*) Eat it? You joke? Disgraziato! You should thank you lucky stars you still got a father, be Jesus! I never had a father to tell me. Don't say you father never told you.

Tony. Pop... I remember everything you say, even when I'm making love. (*Pop steps in, attentive.*) Once I stopped in the middle of an orgasm, the girl says, "What's wrong?" and I go, "You. You left the toilet seat up!"

Pop. (*Pause. Not realizing he's been had.*) Ma tu sei pazzo! (*Sitting next to* Tony.) Who is this girl?

Tony. Just a figure of speech.

Pop. A nice figure?

Tony. Right.

Pop. She go to church?

Tony. No.

Pop. Italian girl?

Tony. No.

Pop. Jewish? (*Beat.*) Jewish is ok. (*Wobbles a skeptical hand.*) Good with the dollars. (*Motioning to ceiling.*) Sometimes I think you mother's Jewish...

Tony. There's no girl, Pop. I...

Pop. First there's a girl then there's no girl. Imbroglióne! You better settle down.

Tony. When I find the *right one.*

Pop. Quale right one? There's no such-ah thing. It's a question of which is the best mistake. Capisci? So find you'self a rich mistake.

Tony. Ok. First thing in the morning.

Pop. Chi dorme non 'pilgia' pesce.

Tony. Pop, I haven't been asleep. (*Loud dog barking next door.*) For the last year I-

Pop. (*Going to window.*) Sta' zitto! Animale! I told them get rid of that dog or, be Jesus, I'll call the police. (*Barking.*) First the kids then the dog in and out, screamin', bangin' doors, barkin' their brains out. I can't sit in peace two minutes to read the paper on the porch, and that dog comes through the fence, shits in you mother's tomatoes, wipes his ass on the basílico e scappato! Mal educato!

Tony. Kids and dogs'll keep you young.

Pop. Quale young? Senti. (*Going to* TONY.) The people next door, when you see them, don't talk to them. (*Hooking wrist along waist.*) pass them by. (*More barking.*) Zitto, strunza! Animale! Porco! (*Enter Mom in black housedress and flats.*)

Mom. (*Constrained.*) Che succede? What is this, the end of the world? Non gridare. You want the neighbors to think you're crazy? (*Pulls down shade.*)

Pop. (*Rising shade.*) Quale neighbors! (*Crosses to bathroom.*) You worry too much about the neighbors. (*Entering.*) I come first.

Mom. Lower your voice. You're first.

Pop. You bet you life. (*Barking. Echoey, within.*) Finisce questo bordello! Disgraziato!

Mom. Some people love the bathroom. They can hear themselves better. Toto, what're you doin' home? Something's wrong? (*Kisses TONY, sits.*)

Tony. (*Pulling away, upset.*) It's over with, Ma.

Mom. Zitto.

Tony. You got your wish.

Mom. Your father doesn't know.

Tony. What's the difference? He loves everybody... Jews, Chinese...

Mom. Yes. With his mouth. Was it her idea? (*He nods yes.*) Good.

Tony. Ma...

Mom. Let her make the break. That way you are free of any obligation. Is there somebody else? I pray to God there is for your sake, and hers.

Tony. Ma. I care for her.

Mom. (*Sharply.*) Because she pulled up her dress! Toto-

Tony. You don't understand-

Pop. (*Returns, half talking to himself, looking for the towel, motions to the window, circles table.*) Cazza d'animale! Non c'è considerazione per nessuno. Mal educato. Mezzo pidocchio. (*Pulls towel out from under Mom; moves R. of table.*) Look at you brother-in-law's dog on Staten Island. Somebody comes to the house it barks once, twice, no more. And that dog, Madonna! Cosi! (*Widens arms.*) The mailman saw the footprints in the snow, grande like a dinosaur, and the mail went to the neighbor for a month! But that dog has respect, educazione. (*Re-enters bathroom.*)

Tony. (*Continuing.*) You don't understand.

Mom. I only understand she's not for you.

Tony. I never once said I love you.

Mom. Because in the back of your mind you haven't gone completely pazzo. You still have self-respect.

Tony. (*Rising.*) Ma, please. (*Stepping through fourth wall into Magic's bedroom.*)

Mom. You care because you have the big heart. (*Lights up in bedroom. Down to half in kitchen.*)

Tony. (*Seeing bike exerciser.*) Hey! There it is!

Mom. You feel sorry for her and the child.

Tony. And on time, too. (*Speaking to Magic who is offstage.*) Merry Christmas, babe!

Mom. Toto, it's time you understood. You can't go through life with your heart on your sleeve.

Tony. (*Taking slip off handlebars.*) I see you're already usin' it. (*Climbs on bike, peddles.*) This is terrific if ya got sciatica. Who designed this seat, the roto rooter man? No. A spiteful fagot with hemorrhoids! Imagine some idiot stealin' this, thinking' it's a bike?

Magic. (*Off.*) Only if he were Puerto Rican And then he wouldn't rob it. He'd eat it! Entering.) The bastards eat iron. (*Hugging Tony from behind.*)

Tony. Mirra, mirra! Cuchifritos! (*Pulls her forward on his back as he fakes eating handlebars.*) Arrg!

Magic. You think it's funny? I had to live with them ironeaters. We move into a neighborhood the real estate value comes down, but with them it's the *buildings*. They're worse than those South American Ants.

Tony. In high school we used to read about Our Latin Neighbors.

Magic. Now you can see them on the six o'clock news.

Tony. (*Handing her an envelope.*) For the rent. How're you feelin', any more nausea?

Magic. (*Suddenly downcast, moving R.*) Comes and goes. Tony-

Tony. If it's money, I'll pay the doc. We'll go to one in the neighborhood.

Magic. I don't need no phony pills. (*Puts envelope on vanity.*) They always give a prescription. They get kickbacks from drug companies. Don't you know that? (*HE looks off exasperated.*) That's right. I'll bet those pills are made of sugar, too. That's your *white* doctor.

Tony. And black doctors are different? They never write prescriptions?

Magic. They're more for the people.

Tony. (*Going to her.*) Wanna know the difference between the two? With black doctors the pills're brown sugar. (*Kisses her.*)

Magic. Well, brown sugar's healthier.

Tony. Ha!

Magic. Oh, just give me my bed. (*Sits. Silence.*)

Mom. (*From Kitchen.*) Lasciala stare. (*Low, sibilant voice.*)

Magic. What're you thinking?

Mom. Let her be. Lasciala stare!

Magic. Have you been thinking about *us*?

Tony. (*Distant.*) Oh. I don't know. Yeah. I guess so. Us. People's bullshit.

Magic. You talk to your family today?

Tony. No. Something happened on the line. Just words. Stupid words. The guys were passin' around a magazine. One of 'em hands me the centerfold and another one says, kiddin', "Show the dumb guinea. He loves niggers." Suddenly, I'm yellin', "You fuckin' ignoramus! Who the hell're you pointin' your finger? Bullshit!" And I walked.

Magic. Bunch of bigoted bastards. They should-

Tony. It's not just black and white. It's Jews and Germans, Japs and Chinese, and something I never knew, the Irish got a thing about Italians.

Ah, the Irish. They've even got a thing about the Irish.

Magic. It's nothing like us. Your mother would sooner accept a fat, ugly Irish girl than me. What would she say if we had a baby?

Tony. She'd call it Sidgey. Sicilians're dark. (*Sits on bed.*)

Magic. She'd have a heart attack, and you know it.

Mom. I'll never touch it!

Tony. No. I don't know it.

Magic. Will she baby sit?

Mom. Mi rumpu i gambi prima chi vaio là. (*Tossing horns.*)

Magic. No way.

Tony. Don't speak for her.

Magic. You're not being realistic.

Tony. Then lemme dream. Life's enough of a goddamn nightmare. I'll tell you somethin'. If we're together I don't give a rat's ass what anybody thinks. Understand? They got this for me? (*Pulls down an eye.*) I got this for them. (*Shoots out a fist.*)

Mom. People don't talk openly. A neighbor gave some drink to a colored man who came to read the gas meter.

Magic. Tony?

Mom. Later, she didn't wash the glass. She dropped it-

Magic. It dropped.

Mom. ...in the garbage. (*Loud banging on outer door.*)

Tony. Who's that?

Magic. Your mother.

Tony. Ha, ha, ha. (*Suddenly stops, considering possibility.*)

Elwyn. (Off.) Sister?!

Mom. If you go back I'll do something.

Tony. (*Rises, goes stage C.*) What?

Mom. Never mind.

Elwyn. (*Enter obviously angry, crosses to phone, punches up number.*) My mouth is so bitter I ate lime and it was sweet!

Magic. What happened?

Elwyn. (*Recognizing voice on other end of phone.*) Your mother's a Bar-bay-jen! (*Slams phone down, turns, paces.*) Back up, Champ. I feelin' mean. When I feelin' mean only one thing cool me, something meaner. Sister, where the hot pepper?

Magic. On the kitchen table.

(*A puzzled look passes between Magic and Tony, who sits in an armchair stage L. Elwyn storms out, returns, holding a jar of hot pepper. He prepares himself, takes a swig from the jar, does a slow burn, puts hands between his legs, curls tongue into a funnel, sucks in a breath, shakes his legs, expels air, repeats action.*)

Magic. So wha' happened?

Elwyn. (*Motions for her to wait, convulses, and offers Tony a taste. He declines.*) Tastin' good goin' down, cumin' out look out! Hm, hm, hm!

Magic. Elwyn...

Elwyn. (*Choked voice.*) Las' nigh...ooh! Drink this and you know why there's water at the bottom of the toilet bowl. Hm, hm! On the subway I'm sittin' so, readin' my insurance contracts, maybe it was two ayem. I just left a new client, you know.

Magic. Uh, huh.

Elwyn. The train was empty except for a couple smoochin', a harmless drunk stumblin' and mumblin' nonsense.

Magic. Was he black?

Elwyn. No. So I say-

Magic. Puerto Rican?

Elwyn. No. (*Glances at Tony.*)

Tony. Chinese? (*Beat. They nod no.*) You sure he was drunk?

14

Elwyn. So I go, "Better sit down, CHAMP, before you fall down and hurt yourself." Well, that idiot pulls the emergency cord. You believe that? Next thing the train full of police.

Magic. You were arrested.

Elwyn. That drunken idiot shouts, "He's got a gun! Him!" pointin' at me. It was so ridiculous I laughed, "Me? No. I don't have a gun. A pipe. I got a pipe," and I reach in my coat.

Magic. Haribob!

Elwyn. "Reach!" says the sergeant, and he steps wide, unbuttonin' the holster. (*Mimes cop drawing gun.*)

Magic. Hm, hm!

Elwyn. Well, now I not laughin'. Those buggers were serious, girl. They search me, handcuff me, shove me upstairs into a wagon. I got one stinkin' phone call and the wife hangs up. You believe that? The Bay-jen! I so vex, girl. I wanted to grab a gun, do somethin' I thought was only in bad movies. But thank God I thought, "Not on their level No! The best defense is no defense." So I lean back and think about carnival and j'ouvay, and how it 'tis to be open and free. But I can't help me eyes. I look around at the drunks, derelicts, petty thieves, and me blood boilin' from the indignity. So I close my eyes tight, tight tight tight, and think about home. Pretty soon I hear the wind rustlin' the palm trees, shh, shh, and then off in the distance, in that early mornin' light... chick,

chick, chick, the cadence beat against the rim of the drum. The first steel band headin' for the savanna. (*Mimes carnival shuffle, and pan sounds.*) From Shah-gah-rah-mus, San Fernando, Sangre Grande, Manzanila, Moruga, and all the way from Tobago! Brring, bring! Ta-ta-ta-tah! T'ousands in colorful costumes, dancin', pushin', pullin' ...all gathered 'round the *steel drummers!* (*Hands high, ecstatic.*) *Sweet pan!* (*In a quick aside to Magic.*) And Lord help you, hm, if your band comin' down the street when another's comin' up. Hm, hm, hm! (Magic: *Hm, hm, hm!*) It's not what you *say* or what you *think*, but how you *feel* and how you *slink*. (*Improvising, grinding hips.*)

Oh, Lord! Hear me hosanna

Bury me shallow on the savanna

Where year long me bones can rest

'Til carnival bands Stomp My Chest!

(*He is now jumping in place, pounding his chest, eyes closed, and head held high.*) Stomp My chest! Stomp My Chest! (*Gradually reality breaks in.*) Lucky the couple down the end say they gonna give witness.

Mom. If you go back I'll do something.

Elwyn. The case come up in January.

Mom. I swear it, Toto.

Elwyn. If that fool punk doesn't show up they drop the case.

Tony. (*Half smile.*) Wha', what'll you do?

Elwyn. He probably doesn't even know where the court is!

Mom. I'll...put out a contract!

Magic. You've got witnesses.

Tony. I'll bet you would, too.

Mom. On my father's grave!

Elwyn. Sister, I need that favor. Two hundred. For the baby.

Magic. Elwyn, I-

Elwyn. (*Going to her.*) The doctor bills. Just to tide me over 'til next week, Friday.

Magic. In the envelope. (*Elwyn goes to vanity.*)

Tony. (*To Mom.*) She's the whitest thing that ever came into my life.

Elwyn. (*Counting contents of envelope.*) Sister...

Mom. Bravo!

Elwyn. ... you know me.

Mom. Bravo! Let her be white with her own.

Elwyn. I not a hateful man, but livin' here? ... is too much a' trouble.

Magic. Elwyn... (*Moving up R.*)

Elwyn. (*Turning with her.*) Even that low class whi... (*Checks Tony out with an over-the-shoulder glance, then in a lowered voice, but continued intensity.*) white came before me. I don't feature spendin' my life overcomin' that foolishness. Not me. Sister, it's a no good here.

Magic. God! Elwyn, please. (*Moving away.*)

Elwyn. Here they kill your spirit, take away your pride, destroy your manhood. God!

Magic. (*Turning on him.*) Elwyn, for God sake!

Elwyn. Ok. Ok. Well, thanks. I'll be talkin' to you. (*He kisses her cheek, starts out, turns.*) Don't play the fool *twice.* (*Exiting.*) Champ!

Tony. Stick around. I got tickets to the Policemen's Ball.

Elwyn. You go. You got the clear head. (*Exits. Silence.*)

Magic. Tony?

Tony. Hm? (*Leaning back in chair.*)

Magic. It dropped.

Tony. What dropped?

Magic. My period.

Tony. (*Stiffening.*) You're...Could you bleed and still be pregnant?

Magic. If it's small. This isn't. (*Tony becomes distant, disappointment and hurt welling up.*)

Mom. You could have your pick.

Magic. These things happen.

Mom. You've got education. You never opened yourself up, that's all. You always found too much fault. As a child you'd say, "She's nice, but her ears are too big." "That one's nose is flat." "This one's bowlegged." Toto...

Magic. What're you thinking?

Mom. Open your eyes, Toto.

Tony. I think I'm ridin' a carousel reachin' for smoke rings.

Magic. What?

Tony. (*Moving gradually in a half circle, speaking to himself, half to Mom.*) All of a sudden the bottom fell out of Christmas. It was like a door in my guts opened and slammed on a feelin' I never knew was there. I guess I looked at what was in her stomach as her gift to me, and I wanted it, more than I realized. This was gonna be a great Christmas, too. Now it's dead, over. (*A new thought, turning to Magic angrily.*) Did you take something?

Magic. (*Coolly.*) No.

Tony. 'Cause if you did...

Magic. I said no.

Tony. Don't lie to me.

Magic. All I took was ex-lax and I told you. I took it because we ate all that crazy food. I wanted to clean out my system before the calories built up.

Tony. You cleaned it out awright, baby! What about that doctor you started going to?

Magic. He had nothing to do with it.

Tony. How the hell do I know?

Magic. Because I'm telling you! He gave me a prescription.

Tony. For what, ex-lax?

Magic. I told you that, too.

Tony. No. You never said what it was for. But that's you all over... tight lips and a loose ass.

Magic. Damn you! You want to know everything. I can't even go to the bathroom alone.

Tony. Somebody's gotta prop you up!

Magic. Ok. They were pills.

Tony. What've you got, a brown sugar deficiency?

Magic. I haven't even taken them yet. (*Taking vial of pills from bathrobe pocket, throws it at him.*) Here. Count them!

Tony. (*Knocking it away.*) Count your ass! I don't know what you did in that doctor's office. It's all a broad's show anyway. Those pills got a name?

Magic. They're to relax me.

Tony. Terrific! Now you're ex-laxed and re-laxed.

Magic. I don't understand you. You should be happy. You're safe.

Tony. I don't wanna be safe! Understand? I care. Do you or that creepy ass doctor?

Magic. He had nothing to do with it.

Tony. Sez you! Flush it down the toilet. Well, I hope my sperm goes out to sea and knocks up a shark whose baby bites his prick off when he's out swimming.

Magic. Ha. You're ridiculous sometimes, you know? I think you're the one who should go around the corner, and I'll pay. I feel just as bad as you.

Tony. Where? In your soul? Which one, right or left? (*Indicating feet.*)

Magic. I'm realistic. You're not.

Tony. Right. I'm still talkin' to you.

Magic. You act like it was alive and walking around. It wasn't even formed yet.

Tony. In my head it was!

Magic. So now we're both not pregnant.

Tony. (*Knocks her down on bed.*) Don't get smart! I'll set that doc up for a bone specialist. He does surgery, play piano? I'll crush the bastard's hands! What galls me is that I still don't know why you went to him.

Magic. Nerves.

Tony. What nerves?

Magic. You.

Tony. Me?

Magic. Yes.

Tony. What the hell've I done?

Magic. Don't you feel it? Look at us?

Tony. I been lookin'. All I see is an abortion. (*Moves L.*)

Magic. The only abortion is us! Where's the joy, the fun? It's Christmas and we're fighting.

Tony. I'm not fighting. You're fighting! It's Christmas? Where's my gift, my immaculate deception?

Magic. (*Studies him a moment.*) Do you love me?

Mom. I tried to bring you up the right way. (*Crossing to edge of kitchen.*)

Magic. See? (*Lights up in kitchen.*)

Mom. I know I made mistakes.

Magic. You don't' talk.

Mom. Your father and I, we...

Magic. No. Not about what really matters. (*Goes to vanity; sits.*)

Mom. We're not perfect, but we're still together. Are you angry because we're not perfect? I gave the best I knew how. The arguments, well, I'm sorry, Vergine Maria! There were times he drove me out of the house, too. I thought I was going pazzo, listening to his way of thinking. How many times I wanted to kill myself. But I didn't. The family was first. I gave up my life, my passions to keep the family together. Sometimes, Toto, I shut myself up in the attic to get away, to hear myself think. The other day I thought I heard you coming home from the park, bouncing the basketball in the driveway. And always, always just when the food was on the table. Ti ricordi, Toto? Now you do this thing to me, your mother? It's like my own hand rising up slapping me in the face. Toto, you were going to bring me honor.

Tony. Ma. (*Slowly.*) I Wanted to die! (*Stepping into kitchen.*)

Mom. But you didn't. For the same reason you never said I love you.

Tony. She made a man out of me. (*Sits R.*)

Mom. Bravo! Profit from your knowledge. She got something, too. Don't underestimate yourself, and don't look back. You care? Better to cry for a day than suffer a lifetime. Let her go to her own. Lasciala stare. (*Silence.*)

Are you still on strike? You think you'll go back before Christmas? (*He shrugs.*) Have you lost much money?

Tony. Couplah thousand.

Mom. Dio mio! Can't you go back? Apologize.

Tony. It doesn't work that way.

Mom. It's not working this way. You work nights. Use the side door. Who's going to see you? (*Pop comes out of the bathroom.*)

Tony. No, Ma. I gotta walk with the guys. (*Mom, turns away, busies herself at the stove.*)

Pop. What about that Jenny-gins? I see him on the TV news his lips movin' but I don't hear the voice?

Tony. It's the strike. TV's out, too.

Pop. Out where?

Tony. In the street.

Pop. What street?

Tony. Wherever the company does business. I'm on Broadway.

Pop. Broadway! Bravo! (*Leaning in.*) The union payin' you to walk? (*He nods no.*) Azione schifosa! The big fish always eats the little fish. Sempre cosi. I hear a song on the radio, ah, I never promise you a rose-ah bush.

Mom. Garden.

24

Pop. That's what I said. Things don't come like food in the fish bowl. (*Mimes fish feeding.*) You had a cousin come off the boat and found twenty dollars on the dock. "Cugino, cugino," he's all excited. "Look! Ahh-merica!" I say, "Si. Ah-merica! Walk. Maybe we find more." For a month he don't look for work. He looks for money in the street. One day he says, "Cugino, I no find-ah nothin'.'" I say, "Cugino mio. (*Angrily.*) Stupidatsu! You think in America money grows in the street? America's one big piazza? You want money in Ah-merica bisogno aprire il culo e dare sangue!" You gotta open you ass and give blood! (*Sitting L.*) How much a reporter make?

Tony. Thirty, forty.

Pop. Tousand?

Mom. Thousand? (*Comes over, sits.*)

Tony. Right.

Pop. Madonna! And every time I turn on the TV I see another chocolato.

Tony. A what?

Pop. Negroes.   ......   Mom. Negroes!

Pop. They wisin' up. The nose is in the book. Soon there'll be no more vanilla and we be shinin' their shoes. They're getting' close, caro mio.

Tony. Closer than you think.

Mom. (*Sternly.*) Toto!

Pop. Certo! How much that Gal-ah No-bella make-ah?

Tony. Who?

Mom. With the pomade pompadour. He looks like a good looking Indian.

Pop. Quale Indian? Vanilla fudge. How much-ah?

Tony. I don't know.

Pop. Eh, what *do* you know? You don't even know why you walkin'.

Tony. It's complicated, Pop. It's not money, but jurisdictional rights over new electronic gismos.

Pop. Gis-ah-mos?

Tony. An electronic device.

Pop. You want advice? You got college. Be a reporter. They get paid for walking in the street. What-ah you gettin'? (*Elongating words.*) Pani perso! Lost bread. You gotta the nerve in this country you make plenty. How much that Jim Jenny-gins make-ah?

Tony. I don't know.

Pop. How about Water Crumb-cakes?

Mom. Cronkite.

Pop. That's what I said. How much-ah?

Tony. They've got individual contracts. (*Rises. Crosses to edge of kitchen.*) I never say I love

26

you, huh? You wanna know about love? You gimme a kid with your guts then I'll know where you're at, and then I'll tell you where I'm at.

Pop. How much-ah he make-ah?

Magic. You love talking around things.

Tony. (*Straddling both sets.*) You go to a doctor who'll rip out a heart for a dollar. What's he care how I feel? He puts the gloves on, takes them off. He's clean. Some fuckin' nativity!

Pop. Forty-five thousand?

Magic. But about what really counts you don't talk at all.

Tony. Then you tell me what counts?

Pop. Fifty thousand?

Magic. Us. Our feeling for each other.

Pop. How much-ah?

Magic. That's first. A child is second.

Pop. Imbecílle!

Tony. (*Blurting out.*) Five hundred thousand!

Pop. (*Straightening up.*) A year? He's gotta some nerve! And Bob-a-sah Wallers?

Tony. A million!

Pop. Manch'i cane! (*Dog barking.*) Cazza d'animale! Zito! (*Going to rear window down of table.*)

Mom. (*Cutting him off.*) Will you lower that voice. The neighbors. (*They meet in front of table.*)

Pop. Whose life you livin', yours or the neighbors? You gonna let them dictate your life?

Mom. There's only one dictator here!

Pop. But why you always take the other part?

Mom. If you heard yourself you'd know why.

Tony. (*In place.*) Coffee, Pop? The water's boiling'.

Mom. People are sleeping.

Pop. 'People are sleeping'. People sleep their brains away, in their nightclothes all their lives.

Mom. And you never sleep. Even in bed you're an opera. Just lower your voice, simple. I would tell the dog, but it doesn't understand.

(*They are toe-to-toe.*)

Pop. Esatto! It has no training. Non sa ragionàre... he can't reason, and therefore belongs in the country.

Mom. Some people belong in the country, too. I made a simple request. No need for a federal case. Lower your voice. You're too loud.

(*They are nose-to-nose.*)

Pop. (*Shouting.*) Quale loud?! (*Mom leans back covering her ears.*) You don't know what loud is!

Mom. I don't? I'm married to it forty years. And for one morning in my life I'd like a little peace and quiet.

Pop. (*Gesturing, hand in air, moving above table.*) There'll be plenty peace and quiet when we're dead, and be Jesus, I'm not dead yet.

Magic. Do you love me? (*Tony stares into bedroom.*)

Pop. To be alive is to talk, to express, to discuss. (*Mom crosses up R. of table, mimes chatterbox with hands.*) And then, when you dead in the coffin, cosi, (*Falls on table, arms stretched out, looking straight ahead.*) morte per l'eternità, they cry over you body... piangono la perdita di quel grand'uomo! Speak, speak, speeek to me!

Mom. (*Leaning on table along side POP head slightly higher.*) Lacrime di coccodrillo! Nobody will cry for you to speak. We'll hear that voice long after *we're* dead!

Tony. Ha, ha, ha!

Pop. Comincia, eh? (*Turning in place to face MOM nose-to-nose.*) Shut you mouth.

Mom. (*Rising a little.*) Shut yours.

Pop. (*Rising to her level.*) I'm the husband.

Mom. (*Rising above him.*) And I'm the wife.

Tony. Ma.

Magic. Do you love me?

Pop. (*Rising to her level.*) The husband comes first!

Tony. Pop.

Mom. (*Straightening up.*) Not when he's wrong.

Magic. Do you love me?

Pop. (*Straightening up.*) Right or wrong!

Mom. This is not Russia!

Tony. (*To MAGIC.*) You trying to get back at whitey through my kid?

Elwyn. (*A vision in MAGIC'S mind; down L., speaking firmly.*) They broke your heart once. Remember? *I* took you to the hospital, bleeding, the pain in your gut.

Magic. (*Turning on TONY.*) Are you crazy?

Pop. You're a woman who loves trouble!

Mom. Like you love silence.

Elwyn. The child came, not a whisper from the grandparents.

Magic. I think you are crazy.

Elwyn. He doesn't understand. Cut 'im loose!

Magic. You realize what it means to bring a child in this world?

Elwyn. Let 'im feel the fire!

Pop. Puttana, Gesù Cristo!

Magic. ...the sacrifice?

Mom. You'll get paid for that mouth.

Magic. And on a prayer that you might love me?

Mom. One day you'll bust a vein! (*Overlapping voices.*)

Pop. Zittati, I say! (*Banging table.*)

Mom. You, you, you!

Pop. Disgraziato!

Mom. Damn you! You shut up! You don't know what a puttana is!

Tony. Ma. Go upstairs.

Mom. Tell him! If you were married to a puttana you'd know.

Tony. Ma!

Magic. When I was married I never saw my husband's people.

Mom. Open that fat mouth with a puttana-

Magic. To them I was *black*.

Mom. ...and find yourself in the street!

Magic. A piece of *dirt!* I saw them for the first time when we buried him.

Mom. I'm not that dog you're talking to.

Elwyn. The baby!

Magic. The other day I got a *Christmas* card.

Pop. Benedetto del Dio...

Magic. Suddenly they want to visit.

Pop. San Giuseppe, Sant'Antonio...

Mom. Invoke all the saints!

Magic. Now they realize...

Mom. But they won't help.

Magic. I've got their only surviving male.

Mom. No.

Magic. Even if he is part *black*.

Mom. Not when God pays you back in hell for that filthy mouth!

Pop. Disgraziato!

Tony. Pop!

Pop. Cazzo di Pop!

Magic. And you want me to go through all that shit again?

Pop. You mother has the habit of stickin' her nose where it don't belong.

Elwyn. (*Fading out.*) Don't play the fool twice.

Magic. Not me. Uh, uh. No.

Pop. I'm the husband.

Magic. I'm a human being, too.

Pop. The father.

Magic. Comes Christmas I feel like anybody else.

Elwyn. He got the clear head.

Pop. What I say in this house is the *Law!*

Magic. Why should I be treated like a nobody?

Elwyn. ...the clear head. (*Exit.*)

Pop. I say shut up-

Magic. (*Tearful.*) I'm not a nobody! I'm not!

Pop. It's-ah shut up-

Magic. My head is clear.

Pop. ... e finito!

Mom. (*Coolly.*) Some people, when they wake up in the morning, the first thing they open is their mouth.

Pop. (*Fuming.*) Vergine Immacolata!

Mom. Il diavolo fa le pentole ma non i coperchi- *truth will out.*

Pop. In all this mighty world non c'è nessuna come tu!

Mom. And after that mouth God broke the mold. (*Exiting, stops and turns.*) No. He built the Grand Canyon! (*Exits slamming door.*)

Pop. Vai, vai to the attic and hang you-self!
(*Exits into bathroom slamming door.*)

Magic. (*Crossing to bed.*) Goddamn all you
white-

Tony. (*Going to her.*) Don't lump me in there!

Magic. Why shouldn't I? I don't know how you
really feel. With each of us there are two people.
The one outside that says things, and the one
inside that thinks something else. Until I see
that *inner* person I don't commit myself.

Tony. I bare my ass, but you play it safe, no
commitments?

Magic. My only commitment is my child. He
loves me. There is no doubt between us. I've
waited to hear from you, anything. Even in
a moment of passion people say things they
may never say again, but you, you never say
anything.

Tony. (*Trying to understand.*) Ok. You're right.
But you've got a mouth, too. I tried to give. I got
you these things, this apartment.

Magic. Chum change.

Tony. What?

Magic. Fry bait. Pennies.

Tony. This is pennies? Then I'll smash it!
(*Knocks over the carnival hat.*)

Magic. Love is not measured by possessions.

Tony. Oh, that's beautiful! What then? This? (*Grabs wrist in phallic symbol.*)

Magic. You're ridiculous.

Tony. Don't horseshit me. (*New thought.*) You got some creep on the line? Go on. He'll take you for a ride *all the way*...back to where I met you, that roach infested shithouse!

Magic. There are roaches here, too.

Tony. And on Park Avenue, but when you come home nights you don't find the furniture re-arranged. Frankly, I don't give a shit where you go. Go with your kid for all I care.

Magic. (*Slapping out at him.*) Watch that filthy mouth!

Tony. (*Grabbing her wrist in mid-air.*) He's getting the only commitment here. (*Shoving her away.*)

Magic. Sometimes you talk and it's like boulders landing on my head. We start one place and end up... I don't know where.

Tony. (*Sitting.*) Neither do I. (*Silence.*)

Magic. Maybe we need a break.

Tony. What?

Magic. We've been together a long time.

Tony. So?

Magic. So maybe we need a break.

Tony. Is that right? (*Beat.*) Tell me something. Why'd you split from the guy you were going with when we met?

Magic. He wasn't giving me what I needed.

Tony. No? Hm. You walked on your husband before he died, your last boyfriend wasn't giving you what you needed, and now you need a break from me. Exactly what do you need?

Magic. I don't know. When you're *away* I think about you. When you're *here* I want to be alone.

Tony. Come again?

Magic. You're not the same person I imagine you are.

Tony. Maybe I *should* walk. (*Pop comes out of bathroom, sits at kitchen table.*)

Magic. We could still see each other. (*Going to him.*)

Tony. (*Stopping her with a raised hand.*) Maybe. (*Pause.*) Here I am in the middle of my things in an apartment we just moved into, and suddenly I'm a stranger here. I feel like a goddamn fool.

Pop. You don't know, caro mio.

Magic. Please, try to understand.

Pop. You never been married.

Magic. I'm not sure of what I feel...

Pop. Still a puppy.

Magic. ...or what I should do. Can you understand? If you're honest with yourself you'll see that deep down you feel the same doubts and fears about us as I do. One day a Christmas will come and-

Pop. Capisci il sangue?

Magic. ...you won't go home because you can't take me or your kids.

Pop. The blood?

Magic. You'll feel it then and you'll hate me.

Tony. I'll never hate you.

Pop. You can't change the blood.

Tony. But I'm funny about honesty, fidelity, respect. I don't forgive easily.

Magic. Tony, I don't know what's wrong. Sometimes I feel white people closing in on me like the walls, and I wonder what kind of a mistake God made when He created them. Other times, I feel guilty bein' so hateful because I know there are some who might be my friend, a true friend.

Tony. Am I one?

Magic. I don't know. What do any of us really know about each other? I don't know what you'd do in a crisis.

Tony. (*Annoyed.*) What're you talking about?

Magic. You don't understand, Tony. The majority's with you.

Tony. What majority? I'm Italian.

Magic. You're white in a white country. That's the majority. I feel it just walking into a room, in the movement of the eyes or somebody'll talk to me usin' the latest, lazy mouth black jargon, and immediately I know them. Maybe it's just a pinch to you, but for me the pain goes deeper. I think people like us are doomed, can never be, not in our lifetime.

Tony. Bull.

Magic. Tony-

Tony. We can make it. (*Caressing her.*)

Magic. Don't. Please.

Tony. Let's work it out, babe. (*Guiding her onto the bed. In the middle of love making POP's voice breaks in.*)

Pop. You mother knows how I am. Why she starts?

Tony. (*Not looking up.*) You left the toilet seat up.

Pop. She knows.

Tony. Women are the ruination of the world.

Pop. (*Rising.*) The blood rises, and I can't stop, benedetto del Dio! You want toast?

Tony. Burn me an end piece.

Pop. (*Crosses to stove.*) Black is good for the digestion.

Tony. Mmmm.

Pop. It burns out the mustards and poisons. Certo. The bowels come first. (*While preparing toast, he looks in garbage pail, retrieves toothbrush, which he spits on and cleans.*) I learn the hard way. Believe you-me, the misery of this mighty world is the result of constipation. When you go you push-ah (*Gesturing with toothbrush.*)

Tony. (*Looking up.*) What?

Pop. Push, strain.

Tony. Not now, Pop. (*Resumes love making.*)

Pop. Don't be ashamed. I'm you father. Look at Nixon. Sempre faccia brutta. (*Mimes Nixon scowl.*) Why? Cazza di Watergate? Nooo. He's not regular. When you not regular you don't think straight. You *nasty!* (*Scowls.*) When you go last? (*Places toothbrush on stove.*)

Tony. I don't know.

Pop. You don't feel backed up?

Tony. I guess so.

Pop. You gotta gas?

Magic. Tony-

Tony. Gimme the coffee, will ya?

Pop. (*Crossing to table with coffee.*) Half a cup è basta. Then go shit in the park. Let-ah the city pay this time. (*Sits C.*)

Magic. You've got a black spec on your chin.

Tony. Where?

Magic. There.

Tony. You're rubbing off on me.

Magic. We're rubbing off on each other. (*Tony laughs to himself.*) What?

Tony. I was thinking of your old apartment. That Puerto Rican super who put on the steam one night in August. They fry *everything*. (*THEY laugh. A moment of togetherness passes between them.*)

Magic. Remember when we played drunk in Chinatown, drinkin' out of an empty brown bag? (*THEY roll laughing.*)

Tony. (*After a moment, earnestly.*) I want you to know something. From the first time we met I never thought of you as black. (*Magic shoves him away.*) What?

Magic. (*Crossing up, turning on him.*) Don't patronize me.

Tony. (*Confused.*) What're you talking about?

Magic. I am black.

Tony. Not to me. I only see the woman.

Magic. The two are the same. You see my skin? It's black and I love it. I'm proud. (*Emotional.*) I love being me. It's the living here that's no good. Here they teach you to hate, to hate even your own body. They want you to feel like a nobody, less than an animal. Am I a nobody, not worthy of even the respect shown a common dog? I don't feel like a nobody. God damn you honkies! I'm not a nobody! I'm not! I'm proud! (*Falls on bed.*)

Tony. (*Catching her emotion.*) What can I say?

Magic. What good's it do to build a hope and find disappointment? I want to die! I really want to die!

Tony. (*Leaving her side, suddenly wheeling on POP; crossing Up c., bitterly.*) One day I'm going to surprise you, Pop! I'm gonna bring someone into this *sacred white temple* who cooks soul food.

Pop. Cold food?

Tony. No. Soul food! Ya dig? Down home, country cookin'.

Pop. Ah, pasta fah-soul! Si.

Tony. No. Damn it! Pig tails, pig ears, pig feet- (*Waving fist.*)

Pop. (*Rising.*) In a pig's eye!

Tony. Pigeon peas, rice...

Pop. This is not a garbage can! (*Pats stomach.*)

41

Tony. Cal-ah-loo.

Pop. You wanna *soul food? (Toe-to-toe with TONY.)*

Tony. Roti!

Pop. Antipasto! (*Waving fist.*)

Tony. Curry goat! Curry conks!

Pop. Cuto-letto! Capu-zella!

Tony. Bah-jee! Mon-fango!

Pop. Mon-fangoo *culo!* Cazza di mare! Lasagna! Insalada! The only thing black is the olives! (*Beat.*) And you talkin' pig-ah tails? Vai via! Eh, caro mio. You got life in your hands and you don't know it. When I was you age I went dancin' all over, the Aragon-ah, Rose-ah-land-ah Ballroom 'til three, four in the morning. I once give Paul Whiteman a bottle of champagne.

Tony. That's *you!* We're not all made for *dancin'!* (*Sits table R.*)

Pop. It's not the dancin'. It's the principle, to get out, to open up, be sociable and stop dreamin'. Today they don't dance anyway. Rockin' their brains, shakin' their culo. (*Mimes rock dance.*) Tuck, tuck-ah too. Yuck-ah-dee yuck-ah-do! (*Turning in place, thrusting his rear end out comically.*) That's not-ah dancin'. That's i pulici! (*Scratches himself.*) Tutti sciancati, nervosi, pazzo, fricassea! Non elegànte. Capisci? Dancin' is elegance. Not Africano. Cosi, caro mio. (*Performs tango with invisible partner, humming, twisting, turning, gracefully dipping.*) Bah rump, bump, bump bump! Bah rump, rump, bump, bump! (*Etc.*) I was a Valentino! (*Stops middle of a dip.*) Then I met you mother. Goodbye Valentino! (*Gestures throwing out garbage.*) Senti, figlio mio. (*Wistful, counseling, sits next to TONY.*) Life, how you say? La vita è un'affacciata di finestre. Passa com'una lucciola di notti. Capisci what I'm tellin' you? Life is a ...glance from the window. It passes like a firefly in the night. Before you know it, sparisci. It-ah disappears, gone, finito, and you an old man with nothin' to show. So get on the stick. Stop dreamin', livin' like a zingaro- a gypsy.

Tony. (*Intensely.*) I'm not. I've been trying to tell you that I've been going with a West Indian.

Pop. I understand. Settle down. Find somebody in the East.

Tony. (*Rises.) Goddamnit, Pop! Please. (Turns away, tearful.*) Jesus Christ in heaven!

Pop. Calma, caro mio. You break you mother's heart.

Tony. Pop, it's me now. My heart.

Pop. She'll blame me, but it's her fault.

Tony. Pop...

Pop. You be in trouble all you life.

Tony. I'm in trouble now. You know why I don't go dancin'? I've been up on that windowsill, a mumma luca like the cat. And why? I've been beaten down, Pop. Ever since I was a kid Mama'd say, "You can do better than that." Better than what, Pop? Marylin Monroe? When I needed you, you were either working or fighting over some inconsequential bullshit chip in the sink. Even now I try talking to you and I get a goddamn song and dance about a *toilet seat!*

Pop. What-ah you talkin'? I took you kids to the best zoos.

Tony. Pop, please. Look me in the face for once in my life and talk to me. I'm strapped. Understand? I don't know what to do.

Pop. I can't-ah tell you.

Tony. (*Sits.*) For crissake!

Pop. Listen to you father, Toto. People have not yet learned to love and respect one another, and so troubles will never end. America is a baby. Capisci? They tryin' to make a fine minestrone here. Celery, carrots, acini pepe… not everybody puts in the same thing because not everybody's you and me. Tastes are different. Capisci? The baby spits it out. It doesn't know that it's good. Too much at once, but piano, piano it will learn to love that minestrone.

Tony. But you and me, Pop, we already like minestrone.

Pop. Certo! And I love Chinese food, too. But, came the time to settle down it was goodbye egg-ah roll hello lasagna! (*TONY turns pensive.*) Figlio mio, money's important, but don't get me wrong. Family's important. Sometimes the

44

family can do what you can't do you'self. Marry a chocolate and what kind-ah family you gonna have? Fricassea! Where you gonna show you face? With the gypsies in Green-wick Village! (*Rises, moves L., then to bathroom.*) People don't talk to your face, but behind you back. (*Exits. TONY looks up, glances around, rises slowly, moves R., taking in the room. He stops by the stove, slides his fingers poignantly along the edge, finds the toothbrush, picks it up not sure whether to laugh or cry. Examining it, he smiles bittersweetly, goes to table, takes a long look in direction of bathroom, then drops toothbrush in Pop's coffee cup. Crossing down R., he stops above the phone, taking in Magic's bedroom with a feeling of having come home.*)

Magic. (*Looks up.*) Tony?

Pop. (*Returning.*) Drink-ah you coff... Toto? (*Looks around.*)

Tony. I love you.

Pop. (Sees toothbrush in his cup; reacts with disbelief.) Toto!

Magic. I love you.

Pop. It's-ah *her* fault. (*Shaking fist at ceiling.*) You never taught him Italian! (*Mockingly.*) Sempre, inglese! Cazza d'America! (*Dog barking next door.*) Cazza d'animale! Silenzio, mal educato!

Mom. (*Off.*) Will you shut that fat mouth? The neighbors!

Pop. You hear me, but not that dog?

Mom. I hear *two* dogs!

Pop. Commincia, eh? (*MAGIC and TONY move toward each other. POP girds for battle, exiting.*) Whose life you livin', yours or the neighbors? (*Voice trails off; kitchen lights dim out.*) I'm-ah the husband, THE LAW! When I say shut up, it's-ah shut up, and be Jesus, you better shut up! (*TONY and MAGIC embrace and kiss, as lights fade to black.*)

END PLAY

PROPERTY AND COSTUME LIST

TONY—
> envelope with rent money
> hand towel
> flannel shirt, turtleneck

POP—
> matches
> toothbrush
> bathrobe, t-shirt beneath, slippers

MOM—
> black dress
> flats
> sweater

MAGIC—
> bathrobe
> men's wool socks for slippers

ELWYN—
> leather jacket with fur collar
> shirt and tie

Kitchen—
> coffee pot, toaster, cups, saucers, spoons,
> loaf of white bread

Living room/Bedroom—
> carnival hat, jar of hot pepper, bike exerciser,
> divan, telephone

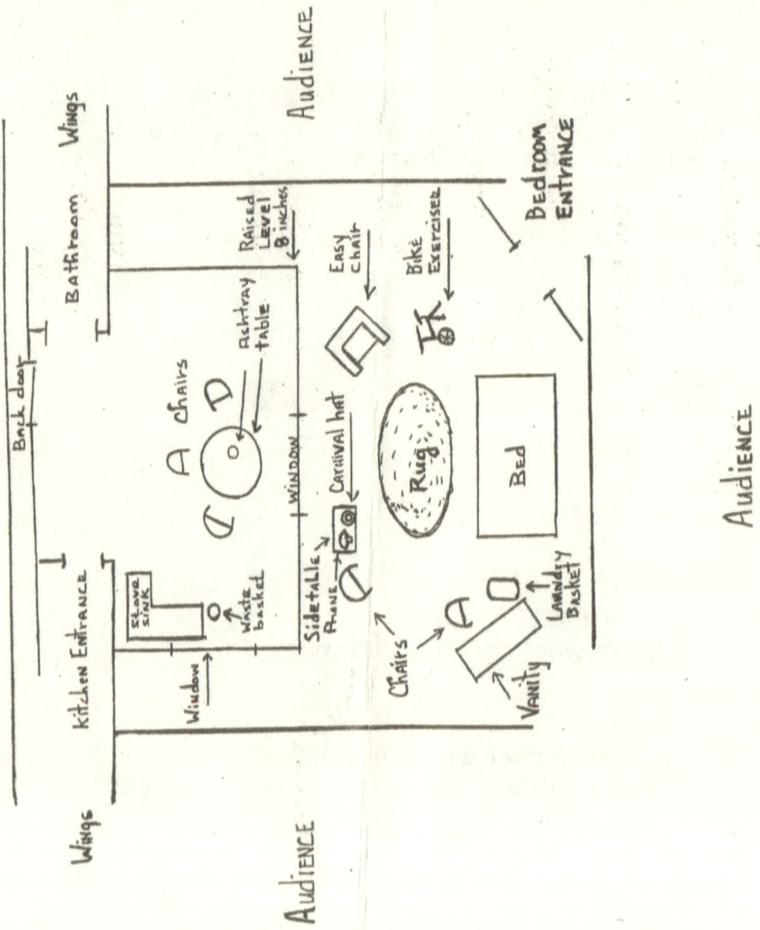

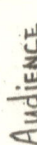

Ground plan for Chiaroscúro as produced in the Double Image Theatre's "Metropolitan Original Play Festival".

GLOSSARY OF ITALIAN
(Some southern dialect)

Africano (ah-free-KAHN-no) African.

Acini pepe (ah-CHIN-ee PEP-peh) Pasta dots.

Anti-pasto (AHN-tee PAH-stah) Appetizers

Azione schifósa (ah-tsee-OH-neh skee-FOH-sah) Dirty action.

Basílico e scappato (Bah-Zee-le-co eh skah-PAH-toe) Basil and runs.

Basta (BAH-stah) Enough.

Benedetto del dio (ben-eh-DEHT-toe dell DEE-oh) Blessed God.

Bisgnio aprire il culo e dare sangue (bee-SOHN-yo ah-PREER-eh eel KOOL-loh eh DAH-reh SAHN-gway) You must open your ass, give blood.

Bravo (BRAH-voh) Great, terrific.

Buon giorno (BOO-own JORE-no) Good day.

Calma (KAH-mah)Calm.

Camina (kah-MEEN-nah) Walk.

Capisce il sangue? (kah-PEESH-eh eel SAHN-gway) Understand the blood?

Caro mio (KAH-roe MEE-o) My dear.

Cazza d'animale (KAH-zah d'ahn-ee-MAHL-eh)
Damn animal.

Cazza di mare (KAH-zah dee MAH-reh) Damn
seafood.

Cèrto (CHAIR-toe) Certainly.

Chiacchieróne (kee-ya-kee-eh-ROWN-neh)
Chatterbox.

Chiaroscúro (key-ya-roh-SCOOR-rod) Light and
dark; open and closed.

Chi dorme no piglia pesce (key-DORM-meh non
PEEL-ya PESH-eh) Who sleeps catches no fish.

Chocolato (choh-koh-LAH-toh) Chocolate.

Comincia (koh-MEEN-chah) To begin.

Come si dici? (KOH-moo see DEE-chee?) How
do you say?

Cosi (KOH-zee) Like this.

Cosa (KOH-zah) Thing, what.

Cugino (koo-JEAN-NOH) Cousin.

Cutoletto, Capuzella (koo-toh-LET-toh, kah-poo-
tsell-ah) Cutlet, sheep's head.

Diavolo fa le pentole ma non i coperchi (eel dee-
ah-volo fah lay pen-toleh mah non ee coh-pear-
kee) Devil makes pressure cookers but not lids.
Truth will out.

Disgraziáto (diz-grah-zee-AH-toh) Disgraced
person.

Divertiti (dee-VEHR-t-tee) Amuze yourself.

Educasione (ed-oo-kah-tsee-OHN-NEH)
Education.

Elegànte (el-eh-GAHN-teh) Elegant.
Esattaménte (eh-zaht-tah-MEN-teh) Exactly.

Faccia brutta (FAH-chah BROO-tah) Ugly face.

Fatti i fatti toi (FAH-tee ee FAH-tee TOO-oy)
Mind you're business.

Figlio mio (FEEL-yo MEE-oh) My son.

Finisce questo bordello (fee-NEESH-eh QUEST-
oh bore-DELL-oh) Stop the racket.

Finito (fee-NEE-toh) To finish, end it.

Friccassèa (frick-ah-ZEE-ah) Shatter, stew.

Imbecílle (im-beh-CHEAL-leh) Imbecile.

Imbroglióne (im-brawl-YOWN-neh) To mix up,
confuse.

Insalada (in-sah-LAH-dah) Salad.

Lasagna (lah-ZAHN-yah) Baked flat noodle.

*La vita è un'affacciàta di finestre e passa
com'una lúcciola di notte* (lah-VEE-tah eh oon
ah-fah-chee-AH-tah dee fee-NESS-trah eh
PAHS-sah KOHM'-moon-ah LOO-chee-yo-lah
dee NAW-teh) Life's a glance from the window
and passes like a firefly in the night.

Lucrime di coccodrillo (LAH-cree-meh dee koh-
koh-DREEL-oh) Crocodile tears.

Lasciala stare (LAH-shah-la STAH-reh) Let her be.

Le donne sono la rovina del mondo (Leh DAWN-neh SO-no lah roe-VEEN-ah dell MOON-doh) Women are the ruination of the world.

Ma che succede (mah keh soo-CHEH-deh) What happened?

Ma tu sei pazzo (ma too say Pah-zoe) You're crazy.

Madonna (Mah-DAWN-na) Saintly woman.

Mal-educato (mahl ed-oo-KAH-toh) Bad education.

Manch'i cane (MAHN-kee KAH-neh) Not even a dog.

Mezzo pidocchio (meh-ZZOH pee-DOAK-kyo) Half a louse.

Mi rumpu i gambi prima chi vaio là. (So. dialect: mee ROOM-poo

ee GAHM-bee PREE-moo key VEYE-yo lah) I'll break my legs before going there.

Morte per l'eternità (MORE-teh pear leh-turn-nee-TAH) Dead forever.

Mumma lucco (MUM-mah luke-o) Dopey, mummy.

Non c'è considerazione per nessúno (non chey kon-sidder-rah-tsee-OH-neh pear neh-SOON-oh) No consideration for anybody.

Non c'è nessuna come tu! (Non cheh nay-SOON-nah KOHO-meh too) There's nobody like you.

Non è buono per niente (non eh BOO-own-no pear NEE-yen-teh) Good for nothing.

Non gridare (non gree-DAH-reh) Don't yell.

Non sa ragionare (non sah rah-joe-NAH-reh) Can't reason.

Padre, Figlio, Spiritu, Santo (PAH-dreh, FEEL-yo, SPEAR-ee-too, SAHN-toh) Father, Son, Spirit, Saint.

Pani perso (PAH-nee Pear-soh) Lost bread!

Pasta fah-soul (Dialect: PAH-stah fah-zole) Spaghetti and beans.

Piangono la perdita di quel grand'uomo (pee-YAHN-go-no lah PEAR-dee-tah dee qwell GRAHN-doo-OH-mo) Cry for the loss of a great man.

Piano (pee-AHN-noh) Slowly.

Piazza (pee-AH-zah) Square.

Pòrco (POOR-koh) Pig.

Pulici (POO-lee-chee) Fleas.

Puttana, Gesù Cristo! (poo-TAHN-nah, jeh-SOO CREE-stoh Whore, Jesus Christ.

Quale (QWAHL-leh) Which, what.

San Giuseppe, Sant'Antonio (sahn-jew-ZEP-peh, sahnt'ahn-TONE-ee-oh)

Saint Joseph and Anthony.

Sempre inglese (SEHM-preh in-GLAZE-EH)
Always English.

Senti (SEHN-tee) Listen.

Sidgey (Dialect: SID-jee) Sicilian.

Sparisci (spah-REESH-ee) Disappears.

Statti zito (STAH-tee TSEE-toh) Shut up.

Stupidatsu (stoo-pee-DAH-tsoo) Stupid.

Ti ricorda? (tee ree-KORE-dah) Remember?

Toto (TOH-toh) Short for Anthony.

Tu sei forte (too say FOR-teh) You're strong.

*Tutti sciancati, nervosi, pazzo. Friccassèa! Non
elegànte. Capisci?* (TOOT-tee shahn-KAH-
tee, nehr-VO-see, PAH-zoh. Frick-ah-ZEE-ah.
Non-el-eh-gan-teh. CAH-pee-shee?) Everybody
messed up, nervous, crazy. Not elegant.
Understand?

Quando mai (KWAHN-do my) Whenever.

Vergine Immacolata (VER-jean-neh e-mah-koh-
LAH-tah) Immaculate virgin.

Zittati (ZEE-tah-tee) Silence.